A **TRUE** BOOK

D0795746

# Climate Change

**PETER BENOIT**

**Children's Press®**
An Imprint of Scholastic Inc.
New York  Toronto  London  Auckland  Sydney
Mexico City  New Delhi  Hong Kong
Danbury, Connecticut

**Content Consultant**
Thomas Pypker, PhD
Michigan Technological University
Houghton, Michigan

Library of Congress Cataloging-in-Publication Data

Benoit, Peter, 1955–
  Climate change/Peter Benoit.
      p. cm.—(A true book)
  Includes bibliographical references and index.
  ISBN-13: 978-0-531-20557-0 (lib. bdg.)          978-0-531-28106-2 (pbk.)
  ISBN-10: 0-531-20557-6 (lib. bdg.)               0-531-28106-X (pbk.)
1. Climatic changes—Juvenile literature. 2. Shishmaref (Alaska)—Climate—Juvenile literature.
3. Global temperature changes—Juvenile literature. I. Title. II. Series.
  QC903.15.B46 2011
  304.2'5—dc22                                        2010045961

All rights reserved. Published in 2011 by Children's Press, an imprint of Scholastic Inc.
Printed in China. 62
SCHOLASTIC, CHILDREN'S PRESS, A TRUE BOOK and associated logos are trademarks and/or registered trademarks of Scholastic Inc.

1 2 3 4 5 6 7 8 9 10 R 18 17 16 15 14 13 12 11

# Find the Truth!

**Everything** you are about to read is true *except* for one of the sentences on this page.

Which one is **TRUE**?

**T or F**   Earth's land is disappearing into oceans.

**T or F**   Climate change won't affect people for many years.

Find the answers in this book.

# Contents

THE **BIG** TRUTH!

## Shishmaref, Alaska

**Inupiat boy**

4

**Pollution is a major factor in climate change.**

# 4 A Grim Future

# 5 Solving the Problem

**Scientists drill for an ice core.**

Ice samples from Greenland show changes in Earth's climate dating back 115,000 years.

**Tornadoes may occur in areas where cold air meets warm air.**

# CHAPTER 1

# Rising Temperatures

In many places on Earth, the weather can change greatly from day to day. Sometimes it can change in just minutes. Climate describes not daily weather changes, but the bigger picture of long-term weather patterns. Weather patterns affect every living thing on Earth. They also affect the rock, soil, and water that make up Earth. A change in climate could mean a change in life as we know it.

 Rising temperatures change Earth's weather patterns and can make storms much more damaging.

# All About Climates

An area's climate is weather measured over a long period of time. Temperature, rainfall, wind, and the amount of water in the air are all a part of climate. Some places have climates that are hot and dry all year. Others have rainy seasons. Some are warm for part of the year and cold for part of the year.

The Atacama Desert in Chile gets less than 0.5 inches (1.3 centimeters) of rain each year.

**The dry climate in the Atacama Desert prevents most types of plants from growing.**

Farmers depend on a steady climate to grow their crops.

## Slow and Steady

People depend on their climate to protect their way of life. All of the world's plants and animals depend on their climates, too. But climate does not stay exactly the same. Instead, it changes very slowly over many years. **Climate change** happens so slowly that it may be almost impossible to notice without studying the daily weather records over many years.

Some ice core samples are taken from thousands of feet below the surface.

Ice core samples have allowed scientists to look back 800,000 years.

## Is Climate Change Normal?

Scientists have found ways to study what the climate was like thousands of years ago. They start by collecting ice samples from deep inside of huge glaciers (GLAY-shurz). The scientists test gas bubbles in the ice to see what was once in the **atmosphere**. They have learned that Earth has seen many major climate changes in its long history.

10

# Humans and Earth's Climate

In recent years, scientists have noticed that average temperatures around the world have been slowly rising. Even the coldest places on Earth are becoming warmer. Unfortunately, this climate change is not entirely the result of natural events. Many of the things humans do in everyday life are having an effect on the world's climate.

**Air pollution from human activity is affecting Earth's climate.**

11

The Amazon rain forest has a warm, wet climate that supports a vast array of plants and animals.

# CHAPTER 2

# Causes of Climate Change

Many things can affect the weather. Different mixtures of gases in the atmosphere can change the temperature or winds. Different kinds and amounts of plants in an area can change how much water **evaporates** into the air. Areas with a lot of plants can reflect a lot of sunlight back into space. This affects the temperature in that area. A change in plant life or the atmosphere may also have an effect on climate.

 By 2050, climate change could cause the extinction of many kinds of frogs.

# The Sun and Earth

When Earth circles the sun, its position is not straight up and down. Instead, it is always slightly tilted. Over thousands of years, the amount of tilt changes. This affects the amount of sunlight that reaches Earth at different times of the year. A bigger tilt brings hotter summers and colder winters.

Earth's tilt determines which parts of the planet get the most sunlight.

Iceland's Eyjafjallajökull volcano shot gases about 7 miles (11 kilometers) into the air when it erupted in 2010.

## Volcanoes

Large volcanic eruptions also have an effect on Earth's climate. These eruptions can shoot huge clouds of dust and gas into the atmosphere. The gas and dust block sunlight from reaching the planet's surface. This causes temperatures to drop. One eruption in Indonesia in 1815 caused snow to fall in New England and Europe during the following summer.

# Human Activities

In recent years, more and more climate change has been caused by humans. Many common activities release **greenhouse gases** into the air. Factories and power plants as well as cars and trucks release these gases. Even farms can release greenhouse gases. Large groups of cattle give off a lot of gas over time. Huge mounds of trash in landfills can, too.

**Power plants provide us with energy, but they also release dangerous gases into the air.**

# Greenhouse Gases

Greenhouse gases change the balance of gases in the atmosphere. Some common greenhouse gases include **methane** and **carbon dioxide**. Scientists agree that these kinds of gases trap heat energy on Earth, like a greenhouse traps the sun's warmth. As the human population grows, so do the numbers of factories, farms, and other producers of greenhouse gases. This means the more people there are, the faster the climate will change.

**Cattle release methane into the air as they digest their food.**

Methane traps 20 times more heat in the atmosphere than carbon dioxide does!

# Loss of Trees

Trees and other plants absorb carbon dioxide and use it to make food. Humans cut down millions of trees every year. Large areas are cleared of trees to make room for homes, businesses, and farms. This means there are fewer trees absorbing carbon dioxide and more open land producing it. All of this extra greenhouse gas moves into the atmosphere.

# Timeline: Climate Change and Human Activity

## 4.6 billion years ago

Earth is born.

## Late 18th century

The Industrial Revolution—the time when factories began to replace hand manufacturing— increases the use of fossil fuels.

# Fossil Fuels

**Fossil fuels** are among the most widely used energy sources on Earth. These fuels include coal and oil. When they burn, they release energy that can power vehicles or heat homes. Unfortunately, they also release a lot of of carbon dioxide. Humans began using fossil fuels heavily in the late 18th century. Earth's temperature has increased steadily since then.

## 20th century

The world's sea level rises 6.7 inches (17 cm) due to melting glaciers.

## 2007

The Intergovernmental Panel on Climate Change predicts a worldwide temperature increase of between 3.2°F and 7.2°F (1.8°C and 4°C) by 2100.

19

Hurricane winds are
often powerful enough
to knock down entire
buildings.

# CHAPTER 3

# Big Trouble

Even though some climate change is natural, it can still cause problems. Today, it already affects life for plants, animals, and people all around the world. Disasters that can be made worse by climate change, such as hurricanes and **droughts** (DROWTS), can cause major damage to **ecosystems**. They can destroy homes and businesses. They can often hurt or kill people and animals.

Researchers say that a warming climate is likely to make hurricanes stronger.

# Droughts

Since the 1970s, droughts have started to affect more and more of the planet. Scientists believe that this is probably because of climate change. Droughts prevent most plants from growing. Also, many animals—and people—suffer from not having enough to eat or drink.

**People take extra care not to waste water during a drought.**

Temperatures in Antarctica are rising twice as fast as in the rest of the world.

As glaciers melt, huge pieces break off. This is called calving.

## Melting Ice

The Arctic, at the far north of Earth, and Antarctica, at the south, are the coldest places on the planet. The land is covered in thick layers of ice. Huge chunks of ice float in the sea around these landmasses. As temperatures increase, this ice is beginning to melt. The seawater itself also expands as it warms. Together, the melting and expanding cause the water levels of Earth's oceans to rise.

**Erosion has destroyed much of the land around this house.**

Between 1 and 4 feet (30 and 122 cm) of land erodes each year along some coasts.

## Disappearing Land

Rising ocean levels might not seem like a problem at first. After all, they are already miles deep. What could a few more inches hurt? But land disappears when oceans rise up along the coast. Scientists estimate that just a 2-foot (61 cm) rise in sea level would cover up 10,000 square miles (25,900 sq km) of Earth's land. Ocean water also causes land to wear away, or **erode**, along the coast, making even more land disappear.

# Climate Change and Food

In recent years, some parts of the world have seen longer growing seasons. This allows farmers to grow more food each year. In these areas, fewer people go hungry. But not everyone is so lucky. The Inuit people live in the frozen Arctic. They rely on hunting and fishing for much of their food. As the ice melts around them, their hunting areas are disappearing.

**Climate change could affect the amount of food farmers are able to produce.**

# Shishmaref, Alaska

Shishmaref is located on an island 5 miles (8 km) off the Alaskan coast. Climate change is causing the waters of the Bering Strait to rise around the island. This small community of 600 Inupiat Native people is slowly losing its home. The people of Shishmaref are trying to move their town to the Alaskan mainland. This project will cost about $180 million to complete.

# Miami

**Some scientists believe that Miami, Florida, and other coastal cities could share Shishmaref's fate if climate change continues.**

# Lost Coast

**Rising water levels are one of the biggest problems caused by climate change.**

**Shishmaref has been home to the Inupiat people for 4,000 years.**

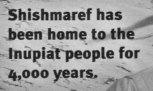

If climate change continues to worsen,
large storms could become more common.

# CHAPTER 4

# A Grim Future

The problems caused by climate change are likely to worsen. Scientists predict that temperatures will rise another 3.2°F to 7.2°F (1.8°C to 4°C) in the next 100 years. Sea levels will keep rising. Land will disappear even faster. People will have to deal with many new problems.

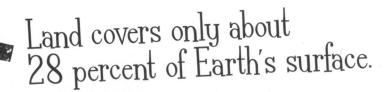

Land covers only about 28 percent of Earth's surface.

# Too Hot to Handle

Heat waves will become a bigger problem in the future. High temperatures can cause heatstroke. Heatstroke makes people sick, and it can even be deadly. Extreme heat is bad for people with heart disease or breathing problems. It can also be troublesome for young children or older people.

Heat waves in Los Angeles are expected to increase 400 to 800 percent in the next 100 years.

Heat waves will be a big problem for the millions of people living in cities such as Los Angeles.

**Rats are known to carry about 40 diseases that can affect humans.**

# Diseases

Hot weather also makes it much easier for many dangerous diseases to spread. Insects carry deadly diseases such as malaria and yellow fever. Other diseases are spread by small animals such as mice and rats. These animals usually live in warm climates. As the planet's temperature increases, they could start moving to new areas and spread their killer germs.

Like many large cities, New York City is sometimes clouded by smog.

 The U.S. Environmental Protection Agency measures the amount of smog in big cities.

## Bad Air

Many of Earth's plant and animal species need clean air to stay healthy. Global warming could cause an increase in the amount of smog in our cities. Smog damages the lungs of people who breathe it. Hot, heavy air also makes it easier for bits and pieces of harmful substances to float around. People can get sick when they breathe these things.

# The Wrong Water

Ocean water contains salt. It is not safe to drink. Humans need freshwater. Most freshwater is frozen in glaciers. As glaciers melt, the freshwater mixes with the salty ocean water. This means there is less fresh water available. Global warming will also cause bodies of water to heat up. Certain types of fish might move to different areas to avoid the heat. This would be harmful to people and animals who rely on the fish for food.

Seals and many other animals need a plentiful source of fish to survive.

By 2080, one third of the world's coastal wetlands will be underwater.

Climate change will affect the many plant and animal species in Florida's Everglades.

# Habitat Loss

As the climate continues to change, many species will no longer be able to survive in their natural **habitats**. They will be forced to find new homes. Land along the coast is disappearing because of rising sea levels. Tropical rain forests such as in the Amazon could change entirely as they get hotter and drier. Different plant species will grow, forcing out animals that rely on existing plants.

# Disappearing Species

Habitat loss could even cause some species to disappear entirely. One animal species already affected by climate change is the polar bear. Their icy homes are melting away. Warm seasons are lasting longer in their natural habitats. This gives them less time during the cold seasons to hunt seals. The polar bear population of Canada's Hudson Bay has fallen 20 percent over the past 20 years.

**Climate change could cause polar bears to become extinct.**

# Serious Storms

Scientists predict that climate change could bring more heavy storms than usual. These storms could cause major floods. Powerful winds could damage buildings, trees, and power lines. Landslides could block roads and injure people. Many areas are not used to dealing with big storms. Residents would not be prepared to protect themselves.

Scientists believe that tropical storms have become more powerful since the 1970s.

Powerful tropical storms can flood entire towns.

# Challenges for the Farms

Climate change could make it difficult for farmers to grow food. Droughts can cause their crops to die. It can also damage the soil and kill livestock. Powerful storms damage harvests. Salty water mixes into the water that farmers use for their crops. The world relies on farms for food. Climate change could be a disaster for the food supply.

**Drought destroyed about 75 percent of this corn crop.**

Plastic can be recycled to create new products instead of taking up space in landfills.

# CHAPTER 5

# Solving the Problem

We will need to make many changes to the way we live to fight the effects of climate change. People are already starting to help. Some are building homes that use less energy. Others are driving special cars that burn less gas. Many people are choosing to recycle and reuse products they buy.

 Americans recycle less than 15 percent of their water bottles.

# Less Gas, Less Climate Change

One important way to fight climate change is to avoid doing things that produce greenhouse gases. Walk or ride a bicycle to places that are close by. Share rides whenever you need to go someplace by car. Try to use less electricity. This will allow power plants to burn fewer fossil fuels. Unplug phone chargers, toasters, and other electric items when you aren't using them. Avoid leaving lights on.

In 2009, people in the United States filled their cars with 378 million gallons (1.43 billion liters) of gasoline each day.

Driving less will reduce gasoline consumption and help fight climate change.

40

**Neighborhood farmers' markets are a great place to buy locally grown fruits and vegetables.**

# Buy Local

Try to buy fruits and vegetables that are grown locally. Although there may be less selection, you will be helping to prevent climate change. Apples grown in South America have to be transported thousands of miles to get to your grocery store. Airplanes produce a lot of greenhouse gases during flight.

# Spreading Knowledge

The key to stopping climate change is getting everyone to pitch in. Tell people about the effects of climate change. Discuss ways you can use less energy and help preserve habitats. If people work together, Earth will continue to provide a comfortable home for all of its millions of species for many years to come. ★

**When people learn about the dangers of climate change, they are able to make better decisions about how they treat the environment.**

# True Statistics

**Amount the average temperature is expected to increase in the next 100 years:** 3.2°F to 7.2°F (1.8°C to 4°C)

**Amount of carbon dioxide added to the atmosphere by burning fossil fuels in 2010:** 9 billion tons (8.2 billion metric tons)

**Amount of Arctic ice that has melted during each of the past three decades:** 11.5 percent

**Amount of carbon dioxide released into the atmosphere by generating electricity from wind:** 0

**Amount of predicted increase in Los Angeles heat waves over the next 100 years:** 400 to 800 percent

**How much the Hudson Bay polar bear population has decreased in the past 20 years:** 20 percent

## Did you find the truth?

(T) Earth's land is disappearing into oceans.

(F) Climate change won't affect people for many years.

# Resources

## Books

Landau, Elaine. *Earth*. New York: Children's Press, 2008.

Metz, Lorijo. *What Can We Do About Global Warming?* New York: Rosen Publishing Group, 2010.

Nagle, Jeanne. *Reducing Your Carbon Footprint at School*. New York: Rosen Central, 2009.

Orme, Helen. *Climate Change*. New York: Bearport Publishing, 2009.

Rockwell, Anne. *What's So Bad About Gasoline?: Fossil Fuels and What They Do*. New York: Collins, 2009.

Rockwell, Anne. *Why Are the Ice Caps Melting?: The Dangers of Global Warming*. New York: Collins, 2006.

Stille, Darlene R. *The Greenhouse Effect: Warming the Planet*. Minneapolis: Compass Point Books, 2007.

Woodward, John. *Climate Change*. New York: DK Publishing, 2008.

# Organizations and Web Sites

### EPA: Climate Change—Kids Site

www.epa.gov/climatechange/kids/index.html

Play games and read more about climate change at this U.S. Environmental Protection Agency site.

### NASA: Climate Kids

http://climate.nasa.gov/kids/

Discover how climate change affects the planet.

### U.S. Energy Information Administration: Energy Kids

www.eia.doe.gov/kids/

Find out more about energy use and greenhouse gases.

# Places to Visit

### American Museum of Natural History: Gottesman Hall of Planet Earth

Central Park West at 79th Street
New York, NY 10024-5192
(212) 769-5100
www.amnh.org/rose/hope/?src=e_h

Find out how ice samples help scientists learn about changes in Earth's climate.

### Dayton International Peace Museum: Green Energy Center

10404 National Road
Brookville, OH 45309
(937) 832-6365
www.daytonpeacemuseum.org/Contrib/Affiliates/FutureEnergyCenter.htm

Check out exhibits on alternative energy.

# Important Words

**atmosphere** (AT-muhss-fihr)—the mixture of gases around a planet

**carbon dioxide** (KAR-buhn dye-OK-side)—an invisible gas breathed out by people and animals and absorbed by plants

**climate change** (KLYE-mit CHAYNJ)—change in Earth's usual weather patterns

**droughts** (DROWTS)—long periods without rain

**ecosystems** (EE-koh-siss-tuhmz)—communities of plants and animals and the environment they live in

**erode** (i-ROHD)—to slowly wear away by the action of water, wind, or ice

**evaporates** (i-VAP-uh-rayts)—changes into a vapor or gas

**fossil fuels** (FOSS-uhl FYOO-uhlz)—energy sources, such as coal, oil, or natural gas, that are formed from plant and animal remains over time

**greenhouse gases** (GREEN-houss GASS-iz)—gases, such as carbon dioxide, that trap heat when released into the atmosphere

**habitats** (HA-buh-tats)—the places where living things live and grow

**methane** (METH-ane)—a colorless and odorless gas that burns easily and is used for fuel.

# Index

Page numbers in **bold** indicate illustrations

# About the Author

Peter Benoit is educated as a mathematician but has many other interests. He has taught and tutored high school and college students for many years, mostly in math and science. He also runs summer workshops for writers and students of literature. Mr. Benoit has also written more than 2,000 poems. His life has been one committed to learning. He lives in Greenwich, New York.